# Breathe into the Knowing

poems

Corinne Stanley

Azalea Art Press
Southern Pines, North Carolina

ISBN: 978-0-9899961-3-6

Cover Art and Interior Collages
by Corinne J. Stanley

This book is dedicated to
the incredible women who
listened and gave me support,
along with their unspoken dreams:
Thank you Lea, Susan,
Sheila and Melissa.

In memory and gratitude:
Ana Roy and Toni de Gerez.

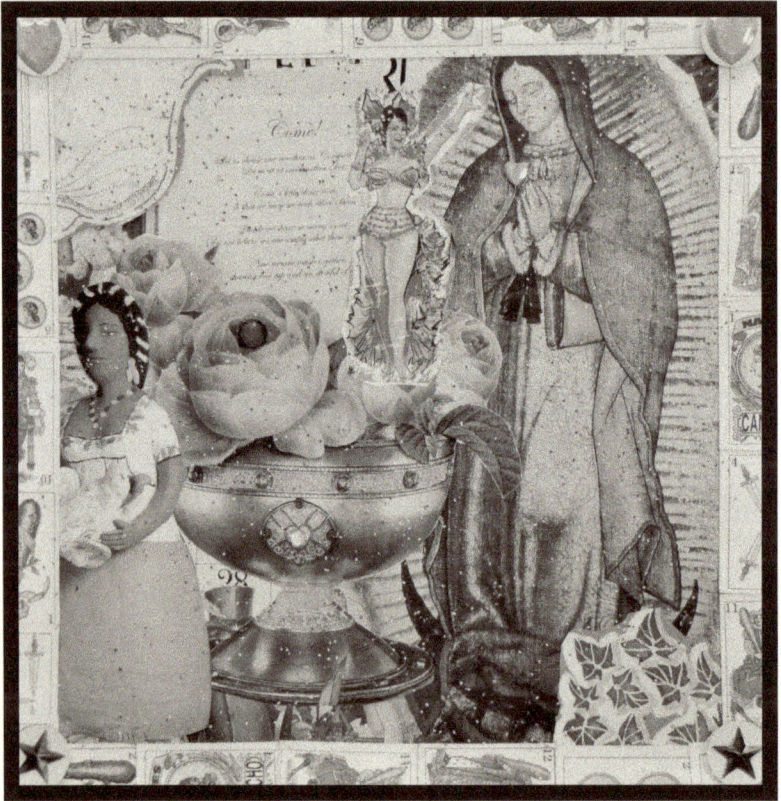

# Contents

*Foreword*                                    *i*
*Preface*                                     *iii*
*Prologue*: The Asking                        *iv*

I.    **Sojourner on the Prairie**

      The Naming                              3

      Face Up                                 4

      Thirteen                                5

      Lake Darling                            7

      Gaming                                  8

      Letter to a Woman Named Camille         10

      Daughters                               11

      Treasures                               13

      Measuring, Like Rumi                    15

      Summer Journey                          16

      These Things Happen                     17

      Fields of Autumn                        18

      Leave It                                20

      Linda in the Garden                     21

      Five Women in a Circle                  23

      For a Moment                            25

      Winter Cardinal                         26

      Learning About Trees                    27

      Persephone Rising                       28

## II.  Releasing the Question

Confession                                      33

Aftermath                                       35

The Metal Fear                                  36

Releasing the Question of War                   37

To You, Those Angels                            39

Transgression                                   42

Dry Spell                                       43

Suddenly, a Bird                                44


## III.  Dust and Light

Climbing the Hills of Cabras                    49

When All Else Fails                             51

In Your Hands and Feet                          52

White Bird, Fly                                 53

Dust and Light                                  54

Living the Metaphor of Light                    55

Into the Wind, Like a Seed                      57

The Messenger                                   58

IV.  **The Kabbala Poems**

The Upper Light                                      63

The Mystery of Aloneness                             64

So Open Your Eyes                                    65

In the Flow of the Holy Spirit                       66

Discover a Secret Here                               67

Go Forth                                             68


**Epilogue:**  The Blessed Day                       73


*Acknowledgments*                                    75
*About the Author*                                   77
*Contact / Book Orders*                              78

BUT ONLY ENOUGH
TO LEAVE THE HEART IMPOSSIBLY LONELY.

# Foreword

Like a "galaxy of stars scintillating through the billowing dust," the lucid and engaging poems in Corinne Stanley's *Breathe into the Knowing* light the way along a path of transcendence.

Taking us from the cornfields and prairies of Iowa to the rocky hills of Mexico, they point to the sacredness of the natural world, its trees and birds, seasons of darkness and light. Each step is measured by a heart that at first yearns to be "tested," then feels its seams tear, as when "Winter is the frozen mother, her lucent breath a lone movement heaving against your wooden door." But when the heart remembers itself, then "Disappointments rise into the sun's mouth, crumble in a fire of forgiveness."

What we are seeking, these wise poems say, is both without and within, and we must "Bring the blessed day straight into [our] anxious heart" to find our way.

With this book of poems at once delicate and strong, filled with evocative imagery and musical cadences, Stanley has given us a warm companion for the journey.

**Marianne Taylor, Ph.D.**

*Poet Dr. Marianne Taylor has been the recipient of the Allen Ginsberg Award and the Helen A. Quade Memorial Writer's Award, among other honors. She currently is professor of creative writing and composition at Kirkwood Community College in Iowa.*

# Preface

Poetry is like food, and I hope the hungry readers of my small book will find a feast within this volume.

I was born on the Minnesota prairie, as were my grandparents and great aunts and uncles. From them, I heard stories about skating backwards faster than forwards and a lone Pennsylvania ancestor who traded with indigenous peoples in a paradise lost and found. I rode my Grandpa's Shetland ponies when they didn't buck me off and gathered eggs in a broken-down shanty of a chicken coop. Sometimes, when my mother wasn't looking, I drove Grandpa's unruly tractor while sitting on his lap.

Later, I was an Iowa transplant, and most of my childhood was spent in a small town with a central square and band concerts on Wednesday nights. I would peddle my sturdy bike onto the back roads where cornfields waved on all sides. I spent more than nine summers working in those fields, and so I learned about the crunch of hard dirt clods as well as the dangers of too much sun and the razor's edge of corn leaves. My youth was about small town doings, that sameness and conformity, but it was also about being completely captivated by nature.

Then came the '70s and the Vietnam War and a wandering that took me to Kentucky and Texas and then Mexico and Ecuador. Always I was searching to comprehend nature as mysterious and mystical as the ancient corn rituals I came to know on my journey.

The collage pictures became part of my journey, too, revealing my great respect for Mexican culture and spirituality. They express my ever-evolving appreciation of the importance of celebration and my reverence for Guadalupe, whose light shines in the Mother of All.

This collection was written over the course of a decade. As I see it, the need to honor and respect nature is imperative for this age. The Earth is our great source of healing—yet we destroy her every minute of every day. If these poems return you, the reader, to some sense of urgency and appreciation for the great gift of land, then I rejoice that my efforts have had some modicum of success.

**Corinne J. Stanley**
**January 2014**

# Prologue

## The Asking

Ask me again
if I break open the fruits of ordinary words,
place them on the hungry tongue.
Ask me if I scope the brilliant mirror
for more than prurient imagination.
Perhaps the incomprehensible birdsong
that colors dawn with bright longing
or a persistent lullaby
that pulls down the bone-weary night but

ask me if my heart took a sudden leap
to when freedom was an airy room,
a stony road leading to the succulent garden—
ask me about the weeping pools
which gather solace for love not
brave enough to be made.

(A dried rose sleeps dreamless
beside a pillow,
a roaming wind unearths roots
sunk in the flat prairie.)

Ask me.  Ask me.
And the light pouring from your mouth
will make these shadows disappear.

# Breathe
# into the Knowing

mething about circles the
ves. Look, the sun is lik
ly minted round gold coin
d does not the moon look
happiest when it is full.

# i. Sojourner on the Prairie

# Naming

My mother's roses hugging the house. The willow trees
    flowing in reverent cascades.

The pencils in my father's plaid shirt pocket. My sister's
    pink plastic rollers on the wooden dresser,

her bottle of White Shoulders next to my Tabu.
    My brother's dented coronet lying on his bed.

The green and brown pool table in the basement.
    My father's duck decoys in the basement.

The trunk with his uniform and medals
    in the basement. How it flooded, how the unspoken

words rose up from the floor
    like a sojourner looking for the light.

# Face Up

Dick Kaylor and the Butler girl
    leaned against an old battered Chevy,

hands clasped
    in a rosary of affection, heads

tilted up toward the star-studded sky.
    The evening smelled of lingering Jasmine

caught in shadowy corners and
    my adolescent yearning floated

into the air like spindly milkweed
    seeking a home.

Later at the drive-in theatre, sprawled
    upon the massive hood of Patti's Impala,

I watched *Romeo and Juliet*,
    held my breath while love trembled.

During intermission
    children in printed pajamas

scrambled on the merry-go-round.
    Patti and Julie giggled about the Sojka boys

while I lay face up to the prairie sky
    and pleaded with the future

to break open my untested heart.

# Thirteen

I was thirteen when I first
   walked the fields with Jana.
      We filed into the towering aisles,

flat fannies tucked into cut-offs,
   long blue work shirts
      flapping at the knees.

The second day we came upon
   spiders the size of our fists,
      sprawled in black and yellow

defiance across the dewy rows.
   Squealing with terror we ran
      to our bikes parked on the road

and left the fields un-worked.
   My father's fury burned
      like the fiery mid-day sun

and spun us back
   before the day ended.
      Mocking our girlish fright

he plowed into the wicked webs
   with a quick, manly stride.
      "There," he said. "Nothing to it."

Our mothers came after he left,
   and walked with us until the light
      faded into grey indifference.

In the evening we clung to our flowered
   pillows, dreamed of colored
      spiders caught in a glass jar.

## Lake Darling

I hear Lake Darling
   is so full of runoff

you'd be crazy to step inside
   those murky, man-made waters.

Yet once in the late Sixties
   ten bronzed girls with

yellow pollen clinging to their chests,
   dark patches of sweat lining

their bright-colored halters,
   piled into the old jalopies

they drove daily to the cornfields.
  Windows down, arms dangling in the wind,

they headed toward the setting sun
   where the wildness of their sun-burnt hearts

set them upon a stony beach
   to be baptized in the dusk of Lake Darling.

# Gaming

On the road to Tama
  I told Gayle, a New Yorker,
how I plodded through the cornfields,
  a bedraggled, blue work shirt

knotted at the waist, my calloused
  hand clenched around a smooth
wooden hoe. She laughed
  as she gazed at the shimmering

fields, her curly, auburn hair
  swirling in the muggy heat.
We were on our way to see Gladys Knight
  at the Meskwaki Settlement

but the sky rumbled meanly and we
  raced to find a place safe
from the pouring rain.
  A kaleidoscope of umbrellas

swayed as Gladys sang
  "It's the little things
in life that count—so Honey,
  put your arm around someone now."

I felt as if I were in church,
  flashing lights marking my salvation
from unpaid bills, my lonely life
  revived by voices humming

in the damp air. After it was over
    we entered the casino and
the earth fell away
    into endless rows of people

glued to the clicking machines.
    I won forty quarters, stuffed
them into my pocket and
    stepped outside into the piercing sound

of a police car pursuing
    the offspring of the gaming life.
A lemon moon smiled
    thinly on Highway 30.

until I opened the front door,
    kicked the mud off my shoes
and fell asleep, a whispering corn
    scenting my August dreams.

# Letter to a Woman Named Camille

I wanted to tell you, Camille,
that I, too, have dug up clay
under the Iowa sun.
A spotted dog scouted the horizon
while I baked it red-orange
on the flat, summer prairie.

I wanted to tell you that I never had a Rodin
but I once had a Miguel.
(In my dreams I saw his wife and child
floating like phantoms before me.)

Those were hungry times.
Yes, that's what I wanted to say,
what all women
with rain-bowed desires know:

you were never crazy
only hungry, and you thought he fed you
until the truth split you in half
(and then you drank).

# Daughters

Lyndon Johnson's daughter
   walked into the ocean trailed

by frustrated body guards.
   She wanted proof of her freedom;

she got her picture in the paper
   and lost her father's approval instead.

All the little girls who were tired
   of the Fifties applauded. Today

their daughters play rock and roll,
   have pierced noses and purple hair.

Now I'm a Seventies girl myself.
   Though I've been to the mysterious Galapagos

and climbed Huayna picchu in Peru,
   I still come back to the only land

where I can lose
   and find myself at the same time.

When I walk into the prairie woodlands
   it's the deer who take my picture

with their large, translucent eyes.
   My father's dead and I never really

had his approval anyway
    so I disappear into sun and tree and wind;

they take me in a tender way
    and for a moment I am the daughter

of every living thing.

# Treasures

Once I carried my hair
   from the *bajio* of Mexico to the
      outskirts of Washington, Iowa.

I planted the strands
   like narrow seeds
      into the rich prairie soil.

Within two years
   the cobblestone streets
      that once diminished

the thin soles of my *huaraches*
   were replaced by the fragrant
      woodlands of my youth.

When I was a child
   I found three white balls
      in the waters of a Minnesota lake.

I took them to my grandfather
   and we buried the soft turtle eggs
      deep into the burning sand.

What is feigned, known, unknown?
   What harbors the in-between,
      of our past and future lives?

My grandfather's wife buried too soon,
   my father buried sad;
      dreams buried in the receding light.

All the dark and restless needs
   that hum and sing low,
      waiting for the shimmering sun

to give us strength, to grow.

# Measuring, Like Rumi

I am trying to figure out
    what animal I have become

to yearn so deeply for
    the shedding of something

old, like winter fur, feathers
    worn in flight. I am trying

to measure the distance
    from when I first

twirled in the rain, mud
    a joyful splattering on my feet.

Cars, phones, TVs,
    toasters and a plastic box.

Take my hand and
    let us go into the meadows

like this—*tadum, tadum*—
    like this.

# Summer Journey

A butterfly weaves
   yellow transcendence
      into a sapphire sky.

A dove whose wings
   hold air and translucent light
      spirals toward the earth.

How to reap such glory
   yet not be afraid of
      the solitary flight?

To know your wings well,
   know your openings and closings,
      your manner of ascent and descent,

never giving into
   a pitiful thought, just being
      wings, light, journey.

# These Things Happen

What I imagine is walking up to you
    and saying, "You matter to me."

    These things happen.

But not in this
    voice-mail, call-waiting culture.

You must be patient with me.
    I was raised between two orchards,

rode wild Shetland ponies and tumbled
    in the towering corn silo.

    You must be very patient

and learn to hold the wind
    between your finger and thumb,

greet the moon as it rises
    into your dry heart

and go with me
    to a place far from machines

and metal confusion; seek
    the staid arms of Earth, green-singing,

"You matter to me.
    These things happen."

# The Fields of Autumn

I travel from the five rivers
    to a city of trees.

Here, under my left breast,
    a tear awakens.

## I.

Yesterday the wind flailed her arms,
a gypsy twirling over the land.
Today, nothing.
The dry, crisp fields
hold empty spaces in stillness.
I marvel at the ochre leaves;
I yearn to know
the secret message of form.

## II.

The corn is cut.
The land is flat.
A lonely sound murmurs
across the vast blue.
Inside my chest
a soft clapping;
wings ready to take flight.

## III.

Fall tolls a warning,
shakes leaves into lonely flight.
I look through smudged windows
for a sign of sun.
Somewhere a child sleeps
in near abandonment. Somewhere
she traces the moon's mouth.

She calls a name. It echoes,
a tiny chime in the wind.

## Leave It

I've left the leaves alone this year,
 curled and crackling in the wind.

They fan their crisp, brown bodies
 across my yard in blatant disarray.

I'm willing to admit that I've
 not the energy and

the excuse that someone stole my rake
 seems quite legitimate.

In the backyard a squirrel noses the leaves,
 then quickly packs her cheeks.

She twirls around,
 sneaks the walnut into her cache.

Together we hold
 the moment in silent agreement.

I won't tell and neither will she,
 why the leaves stay.

# Linda in the Garden

After you broke loose from the walls
    enclosing you into mid-life routine,

after you left your family and friends
    to face the great unknown

why did you step over the threshold?

Now, of all times, for god's sake, Linda,
    you found it—the answer waiting

near the ocean's roar,
    in the flourishing garden of your own making.

What would you say if you
    stood before me,

that boasting smile and spiky hair,
    your graceful limbs?

What would you tell me
    but that the cup was offered,

and you did not refuse
    because of things undone.

The time to tumble into the
    flower bed had come. So you fell,

willingly into the waiting arms of your
    beloved Light, Goddess Almighty,

Spirit from above
 and gave us grief and memory

and a story that will be retold
 again and again:

Linda, who was brave,
 Linda, who was strong

Linda who heard the calling
 and did not look back.

# Five Women in a Circle

Grief spirals around the table,
   a medley of sorrow

spun in the Iowa fall.
   The sky exudes

a musty longing, the world
   retreats into a saffron glow.

In the narrow kitchen where
   five women weep

time collapses,
   loosening a frailty so forlorn

the caged doves coo
   after days of silence.

Oh my friend,
   whatever death is

it is alive, here
   in this tiny room,

pressed against
   the flat cheek of loss.

We weave our hands
   into a farewell prayer

while the lavender light
   reveals a new friend

who stays close to the heart
   unwilling to leave us alone.

# For a Moment

For a moment
the sun weaves a lemon light
through bundles of branches.
Leaves shift and sigh,
lonely sentinels ready to fly
for the cold comes close,
the wind sounds a far cry.

Rocked between seasons you
long for the luminous days of summer
which carried your innocence
loosely, like a scarf waving
wildly in the breeze.

This, before winter tears
at the seams of your heart.
This color, this aroma,
this tender moment drink in,
ingest, make certain
it is yours to keep,
for the avalanche of white forgetfulness
is coming.

# Winter Cardinal

Under the stiff green hedge
    flags of scarlet feathers

urge me out of my snowy sleep.
    I step into the crystal landscape,

an icy breath stabs my face.
    How many hidden rubies

before this world quits shivering
    inside the dark heart?

# Learning About Trees

How well you contain
   the spiral of winter's descent.

How your majesty takes you upward
   to kiss the sky's back.

And your merest movement
   brings gypsy wind and ancient
      murmurings into mute agreement.

And we all drop like
   the golden cascade of your
      shimmering leaves, speechless,

into the splendor of it all.

## Persephone Rising

Abandoned daughter, itinerant sister,
   stolen wife of the underground king.

Not by his choice
   will she awaken to the magnitude

of colors glistening above.
   All for the forbidden bite,

the false beauty of a coveted fruit. Oh, but
   how can she leave, when the temptation

to eat still marks her green heart?
   But rise she does, in magnificence,

eager to burn the forgotten fires
   of the woman she is bound to be.

# ii. Releasing the Question

# Confession

*"Money is money, whoopee. I'd rather be farming."*
Lars Brownlie, ex-farmer, now a security worker.


Once I was riding in an Ecuadorean bus,
one of those shaky contraptions that
stops on narrow mountain roads every
twenty minutes. A tiny woman
hidden in a black woolen shawl
heaved herself on board.
Her felt derby tumbled to the floor when
she sat next to the *chofer*
and faced me.
Tears began to crawl
down her rigid face; the man
standing by her side said,
"We are going to Guayaquil
to work in the factories."

So this is where the heart stops, Lars.
This is when something solid collapses,
becomes flat, like that husband's eyes,
and you have to ask yourself,
"Is this progress?" Maybe the past
wasn't so bad.
You could wake up to the cool morning,
plant your feet
on the solid earth instead of
going to the steamy city to feed the young ones.
That's why you did it, Lars.
We know it wasn't for the money, whoopee—
it's always for the children.

But what will you say
when years later they wake up
to the naked howl of anonymity?
What will you say
when they tell you that the sun rose
like a yellow yawn into a petrified sky?
What will you say then, Farmer Brownlie?

# Aftermath

Here comes Sorrow.

I thought she'd left
to chew on other matters

not my unaware heart.
Here comes Anguish.

She carries a pillow
to lay me down lightly.

And guess who just showed up?
It's Fooled Again, all decked out

in spangles and silky things.
Silly girl, you missed the party

though we'll do our best to include you,
in the aftermath.

These are dangerous times. I hear
so much. And I am

worn out from searching
deception's shadows. He's

a mean one, I tell you,
because he looks so good

until the light shines.

# The Metal Fear

Winter is the frozen mother,
   her lucent breath

a lone movement heaving
   against your wooden door.

And the house talks back
   in eerie cracks,

as if the burden were too
    solid for her four corners.

Quivering inside
   with one thought heavier

than the frigid air, you push
   against the metal fear

of war and weep.

# Releasing the Question of War

The terror grips me
    like a cold wrench pinching my heart.

What am I to do?
    I walk away from the screen,

ask my young neighbors to help me
    assemble a bookcase, give them

hot rolls and toys for their kids.
    I read a poem about hands,

and sit on a chair so soft and silent
    the whispers of my unfound words float,

tumble to the floor and wait
    for me to release the question of

what to do when the whole body
    is in flight from the reckless

actions of distant men. I wish
    I had a hand to hold,

a body to pull close. I wish
    that my dog hadn't died,

that I still lived in Mexico, that
    I didn't see the door open and know

it will not close for a long, long time.

At the laundromat a lady told me,

"We need to get that man!
   He cripples children, he's insane!"

The immigrants slowly take
   the dryers behind my table and

I carry my wet clothes home,
   let them dry in the cool, March air.

Later my neighbor comes over,
   gives me a card she's made

of a woman and child
   surrounded by glittering light.

She thanks me for being her friend.
   Outside the evening

moves in jagged shadows
   dappling my luminous heart.

# To You, Those Angels
September 11, 2001

## I. The Sky

Blue presses against
   the back of my eyelids,

folds my bones
   under my heart.

The sky breaks
   and sorrow scatters

like black rain.

## II. The Towers

If I jump
   will I grow gossamer wings?

Loosen the fire of my skin?
   Or will I become a voice

grabbing the wind like a pillow
   before darkness pulls me in

with a cold, steel hand?

## III. The Search

These pilgrims make no progress
   searching the stinking debris
      for the remains of their love.

Forty hospitals
   wait for three thousand pictures while
      the unborn wait in a starless night.

This journey will not end.
   These pilgrims must find the treasure—
      everyone knows this. Especially the dead.


## IV. October 7, 2001:
##     The Beginning

Lost
   sitting in a room with no light

we asked,
   "When do the engines roar?"


## V. Freedom

Who says freedom?
   A soldier wrapped in camouflage.
      A pregnant widow without solace.

A child sold for a kilo of grain.
   A young girl hidden
      inside the blue tent of belief.

I am the American press. I pretend knowledge.
   I am the global culture. I forfeit the heart.

I am the oil magnate. I am the bank vault.
   I am the weapons factory. I am the invasion

of freedom. Dawn breaks, we are
   dreaming in the house of muteness

and then
   who says freedom, who?

# Transgression

Who will catch the floating bodies
    traveling on the weary Tigris?

Women in embroidered shadows
    mouth their soundless rage.

Men with missing appendages
    crawl aimlessly like ghosts.

Who will catch the floating bodies?

We, the fishers of dead things,
    carrying our nets of iron will.

We, the emboldened liars,
    blinded by black avarice—

we will catch the bloated wrongs
    of our transgressions.

Woe to us who sit in interior rooms
    and fiddle with plastic distractions.

Woe to me who writes on yellow paper
    a shabby concession to contrite moments.

Who will catch the floating bodies
    traveling to the source

of the once mighty River?

# Dry Spell

I am in a drought,
   I walk with dry bones.

Thirst makes a house
   in my throat.

If I could speak
   I would tell you:

My spirit cracks
   with solitude.

Bring your waters
   and I will find a way

to cross this great desert.

## Suddenly a Bird

Suddenly a bird
    sings in the plain morning of winter

a tone so pure
    my light shivers.

I must learn the secrets of winter,
    bend close into the breathing.

When cold numbs my silver bones
    salvation may come

in the tiny fluttering of wings.

# III. Dust and Light

# Climbing the Hills of Cabras

The door to heaven
   sits on a rocky hill in the
      tiny *rancho* called *Cabras.*

So says Yolanda
   who took me there when the
      Mexican sky spread

its mesmerizing blue across the horizon
   and the sun turned a fierce gaze
      upon our eager faces.

Tiny and sinewy, she had
   no trouble on the uphill journey.
      Me, I panted

when the incline rose,
   stumbled on a thousand pebbles,
      my thin, white blouse

pursed with sweat.
   After fingering the indiscernible
      red markings on the cliff wall,

and leaping across a gaping ravine,
   we came upon the hissing
      hello of a coiled *serpiente*

who heralded our arrival.
   Yolanda pointed a slim finger
      at the gate, a hilarious metal foible

with no fence, no barriers
　　to bind the opening and closing
　　　　of our entrance into the Netherworld.

We were after all in Mexico,
　　where the sky topples upside down, leading
　　　　the imagination astray.

We laughed
　　as we eyed the skinny joke
　　　　even my old doggie Buddy

grinned as he collapsed
　　upon the barren ground.
　　　　The next day Yolanda

prepared *café con leche*
　　in a pink casita while
　　　　I carried my heart

home to El Norte,
　　for I had found
　　　　the glittering gate

with imaginary boundaries
　　and turned the illusive key
　　　　that set my burnt soul free.

# When All Else Fails

Try this: renounce the New Age.
   Embark on the path

of ingenuity. Embrace guilt
   and conscience. Shake hands

with shame and sorrow.
   Sit down, all of you, at the

round table of discussion.
   Hash it out:

inheritance, dogma, expectations.
   You will discover

Faith is a rich companion.
   In the stale room of strangers

it is she who gravitates toward you
   and introduces Hope,

who wobbles a bit yet
   carries an epiphany of

rainbows under her arm.

## In Your Hands and Feet

Don't be afraid.
    You are not alone.
        God is in your hands and feet.

There now.
    Let go.
        God is in your hands and feet.

*I had a dream.*

From the dream came the shout.
    From the shout came the mystery.
    From the mystery came God.

(I clapped my hands and flew.)

# White Bird, Fly

Every utterance is a prayer.
    Every word is my petition,

my coins at the altar.
    When I speak, my breath lights the darkness

and I am not afraid.

I have found the silk cloth among the tatters.
    I have reached the golden fields across the mire

and my fingers have let go
    of the immensity of silence,

let go of
    hidden corridors nodding in shadows.

This, so the tiny white bird
    can go sailing, can rise

above the flashing sea
    and discover a trembling, an eruption

of long, lasting prayer.

# Dust and Light

Do we come from dust
   or light?

Do we push ourselves
   up from the dense earth

or drop out of the high blue
   in a stream of brilliant light?

I dreamt of a woman who
   wore an intricate crown of light.

A voice said, "This is you," and I startled myself
   into the being I've become.

If you think life is too ordinary,
   tell yourself that you took courage

when you stepped into the womb
   and entered the tunnel of darkness.

Remember the redbird that woos the morning,
   the loping deer which seizes the wind and

breathe into the knowing,
   live enormously without pity or regret,

like the galaxy of stars
   scintillating light through the billowing dust.

# Living the Metaphor of Light

Pillar of light
  aura and halo,
    star, sun, flame.

The complexity of eyes,
  the refraction of water and sun,
    the moment

between dusk and day
  when grass gains
    a deeper tone.

Passing through the countryside
  your breath turns inward—perhaps
    you are the stretching corn

or the wildflowers laughing
  yellow in the fields. A bird
    suddenly flaps her dark wings,

ignites what is ancient, solvent;
  you undulate with the breeze,
    carry the round form of land

inside your heart. Disappointments
  rise into the sun's mouth,
    crumble in a fire of forgiveness.

Then you grasp this
  astounding moment
    when the tomes of the earth

open wide the pages of day—
    dear God, even the worms
       know how to bow.

# Into the Wind, Like a Seed

There are no secrets,
just you, and the great love
you might someday give.

The world in its slow, methodical turning.
The possibility of sun,
the improbability of rain.

There is no answer
just some thing
that waits silently for your coming,

like the stranger you sometimes
recognize and long to greet,
a yearning and a regret

equal in their patience to be
blessed, then blown
into the wind like a seed

traveling toward the light.

# The Messenger

Listen.
I am interested.

I enter your pores,
and herald the importance of your being.

I eye you in your dreams
with a mirror and a song

and it's a woman singing about
the sea and should you cross it

—only if it's a miracle and
speaks with arms—

Receive.
The angel with no wings.

(Listen.)

# IV. The Kabbala Poems

# The Upper Light

It's a pillar, a ray,
    a word.

It's you, it's your lover, a nation
    a world

the universe reaching into the essence
    of Being.

The Kabbala tells you
    what burns in your soul;

that which yearns
    to draw down the upper light.

# The Mystery of Aloneness

*"If one attains the mystery of equanimity,
one will attain the mystery of aloneness."*

- The Kabbala


October turns to November.
   Where turns my heart?

My days, my nights,
   my longing to be loved.

Indifferent cold precludes
   a soothing warmth. Inside,

outside, inside again;
   the winter birds lay silent

within the milky fog.
   In the deep of winter

the lone journey is
   not an easy love.

# So Open your Eyes

*"So open your eyes and see this great, awesome secret."*

- The Kabbala


Note the roundness of the day, the way
    the wind collars you to the sky.

See how the lemon moon
    melts longing into your dreams.

Listen to your impatient heart, which
    rushes to meet the tender shore.

Open your eyes, treat them as a guest,
    for tomorrow the earth will move

with or without you.
    Tomorrow the waters will undo

what you carefully etched in the sand.
    Tomorrow the roundness of the day

may take a different shape.

# In the Flow of the Holy Spirit

*"In the flow of the Holy Spirit one feels the divine force
coursing the pathways of existence, through all desires,
all worlds, all thoughts, all nations, all creatures."*

- The Kabbala


Six red cardinals gather at the tree
    perched like flaming sentinels.

The cold has bared the branches,
    made way for easy spying.

Somewhere south whole
    villages have disappeared

under the heaving of mud.
    Spinning winds descend

as red commands the day.
    Death or glory?

Insistent life against a gray-gone sky?
    My world is small.

So is my voice.
    I want to weep for the thousands,

I can only cry for one,
    and send into the sky

red birds against the sun.

# Discover a Secret Here

*"Delve into this. Flashes of intuition will come and go, and you will discover a secret here."*

- The Kabbala


Here the blue horse
    emerges from green shadows.

Here the crack in the door, the light
    slicing the small, dark room.

And the invisible hand returns, after
    the grave leapt up and

took you down, far from
    the edges of your self.

Here the cool fragrance of forgiveness
    after the jolting red days of passion.

Here the little white bird
    humming sweetly in your ear.

## Go Forth

*God said to Abram, "Go forth.*
*Go to your self, know your self, fulfill your self."*

- The Kabbala


Silent night, descending
    on a tiny breath.
        This kingdom coming

will alienate you,

and thrust you into virgin lands
    where you will bear witness
        to your self

as you sit by the fires within.

and yours is the heart
that cares most for me

70

# Epilogue

# The Blessed Day

Bring the blessed day
    straight into your anxious heart.

Let no buzz, no hum
    no little plastic device

come between you and the day.

If you are trapped
    inside a cubicle of artificial space

and the outside world
    disappears into a minor beige

reach for the passion of purple
    as it whispers into dusk; inhale

the smell of freshly cut hay
    scattered tenderly in the wind.

Weep for the Woman who stands
    alone, on the magnificent Earth,

in a temple of white remembrance,

# Acknowledgments

"Thirteen" *The Weather's Eye*, Kirkwood Community College, Cedar Rapids, Iowa, 2012, p. 27.

"Daughters" *Prairie Wolf Press,* November 2011.

"V. Freedom" *Dedalo, Revista Literaria,* Casa de Cultura, Guanajuato, Mexico, April 2011, p. 7.

"Transgression" *In situ.* Volume I, 2007, p. 52.

"For a Moment" *The Mid-America Poetry Review*, Volume IV, No. 2, Summer-Autumn 2003, p. 120.

"Discover a Secret Here" *European Judaism*, Volume 35, No.2, Autumn 2002, p. 153.

"Letter to a Woman Named Camille" *100 Words on Mud,* Volume 4, Number 1, 1996, p. 55.

"Into the Wind, Like a Seed" *100 Words on Secret*, Volume 3 Number 3, 1995, p. 55.

"Dry Spell" *100 Words on Water*, Volume 3 Number 1, 1995, p. 32.

# About the Author

Writer, educator and collage artist Corinne Stanley has been forging connections to the mysteries of the natural world since she was a young child.

In her teens, she worked in the cornfields of Iowa, helping to pollinate the crops. Later, she traveled extensively in Latin America, living in San Miguel de Allende, Mexico, where she was taken with the scintillating colors and crisp light of the region as well as the popular folk art and religious icons. Her art collages constitute a deep respect for the Mexican culture as well as a documentation of her artistic and spiritual journey.

Corinne Stanley has published one book of poetry, *They Say This Is Light*, soon to be followed by a memoir, *Daughter of Corn: Coming of Age in the Americas*.

She currently resides in Iowa City where she works as Staff Language and Culture Facilitator at the Human Resources Department of the University of Iowa.

*The author welcomes your comments and communication. You can reach her directly at*:
cjstanley22@gmail.com
319.887.6875
http://corinnejstanley.com

# *Advance Praise for 'Breathe Into the Knowing'*

Like a "galaxy of stars scintillating through the billowing dust," the lucid and engaging poems in Corinne Stanley's *Breathe into the Knowing* light the way along a path of transcendence. With poems at once delicate and strong, filled with evocative imagery and musical cadences, Stanley has given us a warm companion for the journey.

*- Marianne Taylor, Ph.D.*

In her short poem, "Winter Cardinal," Corinne Stanley asks, "How many hidden rubies// before this world quits shivering/ inside the dark heart?" The beauty and challenge of such questions and images inhabit and inform this collection. Her poem "Aftermath" begins with three words: "Here comes Sorrow," and ends with "He's// a mean one, I tell you, / because he looks so good// until the light shines."

I am moved by the flashes of "knowing" and the questions that live together in these poems. They read like prayers and meditations on the sensory and interior worlds that feed and haunt us; they are therefore soothing and challenging by turns. And while I am fond of the attitude and music here, it's the physicality of the imagery that I admire most.

Toward the end of the collection there is a poem titled "So Open Your Eyes" which reads as a short catalog of imperatives—note, see, listen, open—and this energy shimmers through the collection. It asks that we live more fully in the world and honor our own deepest truths, and that may be the only advice that matters.

> Note the roundness of the day, the way
> the wind collars you to the sky.
>
> See how the lemon moon
> melts longing into your dreams.

Note, see, listen, open. Read.

*- Rebecca Wee*
*Poet and Professor of English at Augustana College*

Corinne Stanley's poems shine with illuminating language, arresting images, and a deep connection to the places dear to her. She "break[s] open the fruits of ordinary words, plac[ing] them on the hungry tongue" of her readers, taking them to a place where mystery and faith illuminate grief, love, and all that it is to be human.

*- Cynthia Leslie-Bole*
*Founder, Hummingwords Writing and Coaching*

*Azalea Art Press*
*specializes in giving personal attention*
*to authors who wish to realize*
*their literary and creative dreams.*

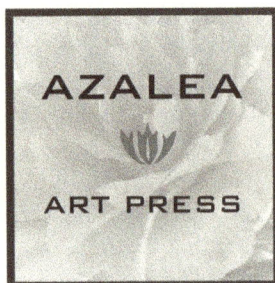

*To schedule an interview or book signing*
*with the author, please contact the publisher at:*
*Azalea.Art.Press@gmail.com*
*or the author.*

*This book by Corinne Stanley*
*may be ordered directly at*
*www.lulu.com.*

www.ingramcontent.com/pod-product-compliance
Lightning Source LLC
Chambersburg PA
CBHW032023090426
42741CB00006B/716